To

es

LONDON·SYDNEY

Note for parents and teachers

The Changing Times series is soundly based on the requirements of the History Curriculum. Using the device of four generations of a real family, the author combines reminiscences of this family with other people's oral evidence. The oral history is matched with photographs and other contemporary sources. Many other lessons are hidden in the text, which practises the skills of chronological sequencing, gives reference to a timeline and introduces the language and vocabulary of the past. Young children will find much useful information here, as well as a new understanding of the recent history of everyday situations and familiar things.

This edition 2003

Franklin Watts
96 Leonard Street
London EC2A 4XD

Franklin Watts Australia
45–51 Huntley Street
Alexandria
NSW 2015

Copyright © 1992 Franklin Watts

Editor: Sarah Ridley
Designer: Sally Boothroyd
Educational consultant: John West
Picture researcher: Juliet Duff
Photographer: Peter Millard

A CIP catalogue record for this book is available from the British Library.
Dewey Decimal Classification Number: 688.7
ISBN 0 7496 5246 2

Acknowledgements: The author and publishers would like to thank the following people and organisations for their help with the preparation of this book: Kevin McGimpsey, Chester Toy Museum; Helen Bliss-Williams, Baden and Margaret Pearce, Alice, Celia and Billy Perry, Chloë and Leo Thomson, Joanna, Ben and Sam Caird, Jessie Ridley and Jessie Baker for the loan of their toys, games and books.

Printed in Malaysia

Contents

My name is Scott.
I was born in 1986.
I have got one brother
who is younger than me.

My name is Howard.
I am Scott's father.
I was born in 1959.
I have got one sister
and one brother.

My name is Baden.
I am Howard's father
and Scott's grandfather.
I was born in 1927.

My name is Hilda.
I am Baden's mother,
Howard's grandmother
and Scott's great-grandmother.
I was born in 1903.

These are some of the toys
my friends and I play with.

For Christmas, I'm going to ask
for either a Game Boy
or a remote-controlled car.

My friend next-door likes playing with her Sylvanian families.

I like playing with Lego best of all.

My brother would like an electric train set.

1975

1950

After school, we watch
television or videos.

At weekends, we often go
to the park and ride our bikes.
Sometimes I play football.

Other children play
on roller skates
and skateboards.

We play on the swings
and slides.

I asked Dad if he played with the same toys and games when he was young.

Dad said,

'I spent most of my time playing with metal model cars. There weren't many plastic ones.'

MECCANO TRADE MARK REGD

YEARS OF FUN IN EVERY OUTFIT

MECCANO OUTFIT

CAPSULE 7

'I had a Meccano set. I made all sorts of models with it.'

'My little brother liked playing with robots and space figures.'

'He was mad about
the Wild West.
He was always dressing up
as a cowboy.'

'We all read comics
and annuals.
My favourite was *Rupert*.
I was given an annual
every Christmas.'

Mum said,

'I had a Barbie doll.
Barbie was a new toy then.
Every girl I knew
either had one or wanted one.'

'We played a lot
of indoor games
or did jigsaws.'

'My sister and I spent hours setting out our farm animals and making up stories about them.'

'I loved pogoing.'

'I took my teddy to bed with me until I was almost a teenager.'

I asked Grandad what he played with
when he was my age.

He said,

'I played with
lots of model cars.'

'I had a clockwork train.
It went round and round
on an oval track.'

'My Meccano set was my pride and joy.'

'I played cricket in the street with my friends.'

I asked Granny what she played with when she was a child.

She said,

'We played a lot outside.'

'We had a big craze for cigarette cards. We flicked them against a wall. If you got one card on top of another, you won it.'

'Every week, we got a comic. I read it first, because I was the eldest.'

'At home, I spent ages cutting out paper doll's clothes or arranging my farm animals.'

15

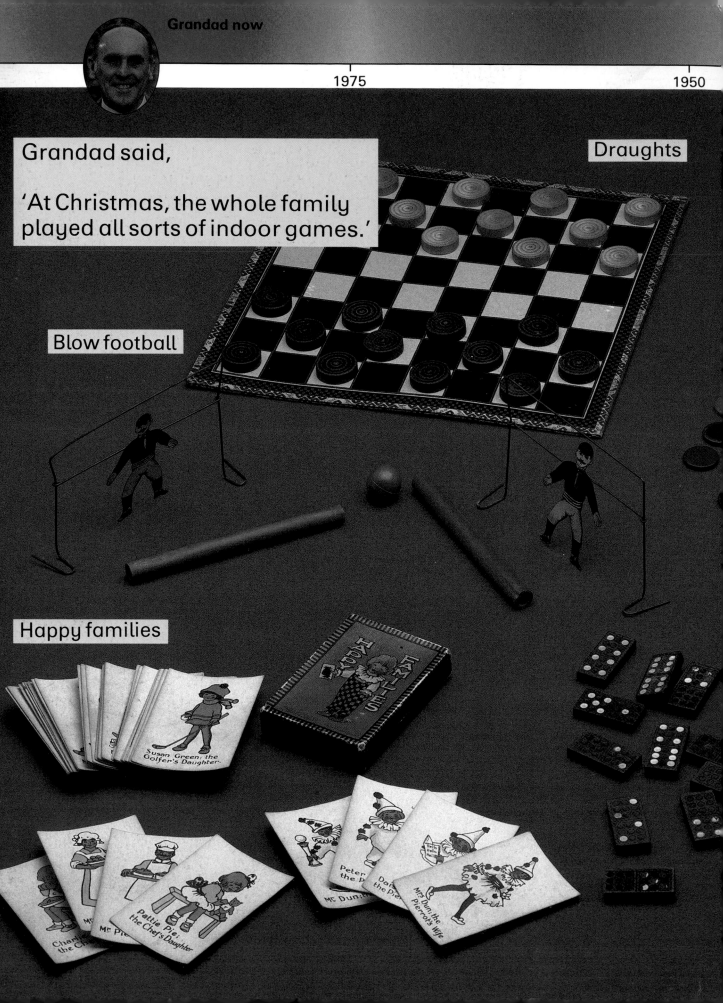

Draughts

Grandad said,

'At Christmas, the whole family
played all sorts of indoor games.'

Blow football

Happy families

Grandad aged eight in 1935

1925

1900

Quoits

'Monopoly was a new game when I was young.'

Steeplechase

Tiddlywinks

Dominoes

Snap

When Grandad was growing up,
the war started against Germany.

He said,

'Children bought
more toy guns, lead soldiers
and dressing up clothes.'

Lead soldiers

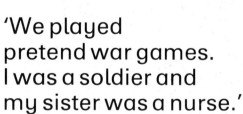

'We played
pretend war games.
I was a soldier and
my sister was a nurse.'

'As the war went on,
you couldn't buy toys
in the shops any more.
The toy factories
made tanks instead.'

18

'I collected
war souvenirs –
planes and badges,
and bits of bombs.'

'I had a spotter book
of aeroplanes.
I knew them all.'

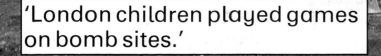

'London children played games
on bomb sites.'

I asked Great-granny what sort of toys
she had when she was a child.

She said,

'There weren't so many toys
in my day and we had to help
our parents more.'

'We had to make our own fun.
Most of our games cost nothing.
There wasn't much room
to play inside in our house.
We played in the street.'

'There was a lot of sitting
on doorsteps. We talked,
joked and played games.'

'On Sundays, we'd skip in the street.
You couldn't do that on weekdays.
It was too busy with horses and vans.'

Great-granny said,

'If you were lucky,
you had a scooter.
They were great fun.
I never had one of my own.'

'The boys played marbles
in the gutter.'

'The big prize ones
were called *glarneys.*'

'The boys made carts out of a piece of wood. They fixed a box on top and pram wheels underneath.'

Great-granny said,

'Some children had wooden hoops, which they rolled along with a stick.'

'I had a wooden top.
The whip was a piece
of Dad's bootlace.'

'My most precious toy was a doll.
She had a china head, which I chose, and a rag body.'

'I always wanted a tricycle.
My cousin had one.
Sometimes she let me have a go.'

1975

1950

BABY CARRIAGES ENTRANCE

'We loved looking in toyshop windows,
but we never dared go inside.'

'I loved books.
My aunt gave me one
every Christmas.'

Great-granny aged ten in 1913

'I always wanted a Noah's Ark with all those pairs of animals.'

Things to do

Look at these toys. What are they made of?

Nintendo game

Troll

Clockwork bike

Picture blocks

Ask your parents and grandparents
what sort of toys they had.
Were they made of wood, plastic, metal, rubber or cloth?

Metal aeroplane

How did their toys work –
by clockwork or by battery?

Plastic space figure

Alphabet tray

Which toys do you think your parents played with?
Which ones do you see now?

Find out what sort of construction toys
grown-ups had when they were young.
Show them these pictures to help remind them.

Have you seen dolls like these?
Which one do you think
is the oldest and which is the newest?

Ask your family which ones they remember
from when they were young.

Index

Photographs: Beamish endpapers, 21(t), 22(t); © Britt Allcroft (Thomas) Limited 1992 5(b); Mary Evans Picture Library 25(tr); Eye Ubiquitous 6(b); Chris Fairclough 4(b); Chris Fairclough Colour Library 7(t); Francis Frith Collection title page (t), 25(bl); Sally and Richard Greenhill 6(c), 7(bl), 7(br); Hulton Picture Company cover (tl), cover (br), 11(bl), 13(b), 23(b), 24(t); Lego UK Ltd title page (b); Matchbox Toys Ltd cover (br); Peter Millard imprint page, 4(t), 5(c), 6(tr), 8(t), 9(r), 10(l), 11(t), 11(br), 15(bl), 16-17, 18(tr), 22(bl), 24(b), 26(b), 27, 28, 29, 30, 31; Museum of Childhood, Edinburgh/Forth Photography 15(br); Nick Nicholson 8(b), 12(t); thanks to Nintendo Game Boy 28(tl); Stephen Oliver 5(t), 10(r), 15(t); Robert Opie 12(b), 13(t), 19(tr), 23(t); Popperfoto 14; Nicholas Ridley 18(bl); Topham cover (tr), 20, 21(b), 26(t).